T0346978

A CENTURY OF
OXFORD

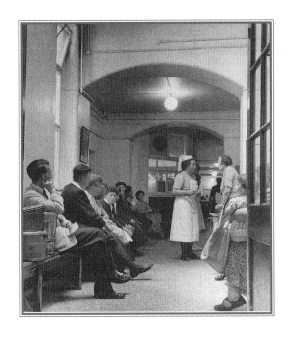

Honorary degrees for Charlie Chaplin (right) and Yehudi Menuhin (second from right), June 1962.

A CENTURY OF
OXFORD

MALCOLM GRAHAM

The
History
Press

First published in the United Kingdom, in 1999 by Sutton Publishing Limited

This new paperback edition first published in 2007 by Sutton Publishing

Reprinted in 2012 by
The History Press
The Mill, Brimscombe Port,
Stroud, Gloucestershire, GL5 2QG
www.thehistorypress.co.uk

Reprinted 2015

British Library Cataloguing in Publication Data
A catalogue record for this book is available from the British Library.

ISBN 978-0-7509-4938-5

Front endpaper: Children playing in the old sheep-washing place in Barracks Lane, Cowley, July 1914.
Back endpaper: Students at Cheney School receive an award after raising money for Leon, one of Oxford's twin towns, following Hurricane Mitch, April 1999.
Half title page: Casualty reception at the Radcliffe Infirmary, January 1962.
Title page: Bus queue in Cornmarket Street, January 1955.

Typeset in Photina.
Typesetting and origination bySutton Publishing.
Printed and bound in Great Britain

Contents

Foresters' Juvenile Tea in Cowley in about 1930. Before the creation of the National Health Service in 1948, many working people paid weekly contributions to friendly societies such as the Ancient Order of Foresters as a way of obtaining medical treatment and sick pay in the event of illness.

Britain: A Century of Change

Churchill in RAF uniform giving his famous victory sign, 1948.
(Illustrated London News)

The sixty years ending in 1900 were a period of huge transformation for Britain. Railway stations, post-and-telegraph offices, police and fire stations, gasworks and gasometers, new livestock markets and covered markets, schools, churches, football grounds, hospitals and asylums, water pumping stations and sewerage plants totally altered the urban scene, and the country's population tripled with more than seven out of ten people being born in or moving to the towns. The century that followed, leading up to the Millennium's end in 2000, was to be a period of even greater change.

When Queen Victoria died in 1901, she was measured for her coffin by her grandson Kaiser Wilhelm, the London prostitutes put on black mourning and the blinds came down in the villas and terraces spreading out from the old town centres. These centres were reachable by train and tram, by the new bicycles and still newer motor cars, were connected by the new telephone, and lit by gas or even electricity. The shops may have been full of British-made cotton and woollen clothing but the grocers and butchers were selling cheap Danish bacon, Argentinian beef, Australasian mutton and tinned or dried fish and fruit from Canada, California and South Africa. Most of these goods were carried in British-built-and-crewed ships burning Welsh steam coal.

Crowds celebrate Armistice Day outside Buckingham Palace as the royal family appears on the balcony, 1918. *(Illustrated London News)*

As the first decade moved on, the Open Spaces Act meant more parks, bowling greens and cricket pitches. The First World War transformed the place of women, as they took over many men's jobs. Its other legacies were the war memorials which joined the statues of Victorian worthies in main squares round the land. After 1918 death duties and higher taxation bit hard, and a quarter of England changed hands in the space of only a few years.

The multiple shop – the chain store – appeared in the high street: Marks & Spencer, Sainsburys, Maypole, Lipton's, Home & Colonial, the Fifty Shilling Tailor, Burton, Boots, W.H. Smith. The shopper was spoilt for choice, attracted by the brash fascias and advertising hoardings for national brands like Bovril, Pears Soap, and Ovaltine. Many new buildings began to be seen, such as garages, motor showrooms, picture palaces (cinemas), 'palais de dance', and ribbons of 'semis' stretched along the roads and new bypasses and onto the new estates nudging the green belts.

During the 1920s cars became more reliable and sophisticated as well as commonplace, with developments like the electric self-starter making them easier for women to drive. Who wanted to turn a crank handle in the new short skirt? This was, indeed, the electric age as much as the

Houghton of Aston Villa beats goalkeeper Crawford of Blackburn to score the second of four goals, 1930s. *(Illustrated London News)*

motor era. Trolley buses, electric trams and trains extended mass transport and electric light replaced gas in the street and the home, which itself was groomed by the vacuum cleaner.

A major jolt to the march onward and upward was administered by the Great Depression of the early 1930s. The older British industries – textiles, shipbuilding, iron, steel, coal – were already under pressure from foreign competition when this worldwide slump arrived. Luckily there were new diversions to alleviate the misery. The 'talkies' arrived in the cinemas; more and more radios and gramophones were to be found in people's homes; there were new women's magazines, with fashion, cookery tips and problem pages; football pools; the flying feats of women pilots like Amy Johnson; the Loch Ness Monster; cheap chocolate and the drama of Edward VIII's abdication.

Things were looking up again by 1936 and new light industry was booming in the Home Counties as factories struggled to keep up with the demand for radios, radiograms, cars and electronic goods, including the first television sets. The threat from Hitler's Germany meant rearmament, particularly of the airforce, which stimulated aircraft and aero engine firms. If you were lucky and lived in the south, there was good money to be earned. A semi-detached house cost £450, a Morris Cowley £150. People may have smoked like chimneys but life expectancy, since 1918, was up by 15 years while the birth rate had almost halved.

In some ways it is the little memories that seem to linger longest from the Second World War: the kerbs painted white to show up in the blackout, the rattle of ack-ack shrapnel on roof tiles, sparrows killed by bomb blast. The biggest damage, apart from London, was in the south-west (Plymouth, Bristol) and the Midlands (Coventry, Birmingham). Postwar reconstruction was rooted in the Beveridge Report which set out the expectations for the Welfare State. This, together with the nationalisation of the Bank of England, coal, gas, electricity and the railways, formed the programme of the Labour government in 1945.

Times were hard in the late 1940s, with rationing even more stringent than during the war. Yet this was, as has been said, 'an innocent and well-behaved era'. The first let-up came in 1951 with the Festival of Britain and there was another fillip in 1953 from the Coronation, which incidentally gave a huge boost to the spread of TV. By 1954 leisure motoring had been resumed but the Comet – Britain's best hope for taking on the American aviation industry – suffered a series of mysterious crashes. The Suez debacle of 1956 was followed by an acceleration in the withdrawal from Empire, which had begun in 1947 with the Independence of India. Consumerism was truly born with the advent of commercial TV and most homes soon boasted washing machines, fridges, electric irons and fires.

WAAF personnel tracing the movement of flying bombs and Allied fighters on a plotting table, 1944. *(Illustrated London News)*

The *Lady Chatterley* obscenity trial in 1960 was something of a straw in the wind for what was to follow in that decade. A collective loss of inhibition seemed to sweep the land, as the Beatles and the Rolling Stones transformed popular music, and retailing, cinema and the theatre were revolutionised. Designers, hairdressers, photo-graphers and models moved into places vacated by an Establishment put to flight by the new breed of satirists spawned by *Beyond the Fringe* and *Private Eye*.

In the 1970s Britain seems to have suffered a prolonged hangover after the excesses of the previous decade. Ulster, inflation and union troubles were not made up for by entry into the EEC, North Sea Oil, Women's Lib or, indeed, Punk Rock. Mrs Thatcher applied the corrective in the 1980s, as the country moved over more and more from its old manufacturing base to providing services, consulting, advertising, and expertise in the 'invisible' market of high finance or in IT.

The post-1945 townscape has seen changes to match those in the worlds of work, entertainment and politics. In 1952 the Clean Air Act served notice on smogs and pea-souper fogs, smuts and blackened buildings, forcing people to stop burning coal and go over to smokeless sources of heat and energy. In the same decade some of the best urban building took place in the 'new towns' like Basildon, Crawley, Stevenage and Harlow. Elsewhere open warfare was declared on slums and what was labelled inadequate, cramped, back-to-back, two-up, two-down, housing. The new 'machine for living in' was a flat in a high-rise block. The architects and planners who promoted these were in league with the traffic engineers, determined to keep the motor car moving whatever the price in multi-storey car parks, meters, traffic wardens and ring roads. The old pollutant, coal smoke, was replaced by petrol and diesel exhaust, and traffic noise.

Fast food was no longer only a pork pie in a pub or fish-and-chips. There were Indian curry houses, Chinese take-aways and American-style hamburgers, while the drinker could get away from beer in a wine bar. Under the impact of television the big Gaumonts and Odeons closed or were rebuilt as multi-screen cinemas, while the palais de dance gave way to discos and clubs.

From the late 1960s the introduction of listed buildings and conservation areas, together with the growth of preservation societies, put a brake on 'comprehensive redevelopment'. The end of the century and the start of the Third Millennium saw new challenges to the health of towns and the wellbeing of the nine out of ten people who now live urban lives. The fight is on to prevent town centres from dying, as patterns of housing and shopping change, and edge-of-town supermarkets exercise the attractions of one-stop shopping. But as banks and department stores close, following the haberdashers, greengrocers, butchers and ironmongers, there are signs of new growth such as farmers' markets, and corner stores acting as pick-up points where customers collect shopping ordered on-line from web sites.

Futurologists tell us that we are in stage two of the consumer revolution: a shift from mass consumption to mass customisation driven by a desire to have things that fit us and our particular lifestyle exactly, and for better service. This must offer hope for small city-centre shop premises, as must the continued attraction of physical shopping, browsing and being part of a crowd: in a word, 'shoppertainment'. Another hopeful trend for towns is the growth in the number of young

Manchester during the Commonwealth Games in 2002. The city, like others all over the country, has experienced massive redevelopment and rejuvenation in recent years. *(Chris Makepeace)*

people postponing marriage and looking to live independently, alone, where there is a buzz, in 'swinging single cities'. Theirs is a 'flats-and-cafés' lifestyle, in contrast to the 'family suburbs', and certainly fits in with government's aim of building 60 per cent of the huge amount of new housing needed on 'brown' sites, recycled urban land. There looks to be plenty of life in the British town yet.

Oxford: An Introduction

A few years ago, Oxford tourist buses took visitors to a concrete over-bridge on the A34 so that they could all, for a moment, become modern equivalents of Matthew Arnold's Scholar Gipsy gazing down on 'That sweet city with her dreaming spires'. The camera-touting tourists leaning from their double-decker bus above the busy dual carriageway wanted to record a seemingly unchanged Oxford from a modern structure; as they took their pictures, they were doubtless unaware of plans to turn the green Hinksey meadows in the foreground into a business park. That scheme was eventually defeated but, because of the growth of Oxford during the twentieth century, roads, houses, factories, hospitals and schools have occupied many other surrounding meadows and fields. In 1900 Oxford was still a comparatively small city with a population of nearly 50,000 in an area of 4,670 acres (1,900 hectares); now, the city is home to over 141,000 people and, having incorporated several former villages, it covers more than 11,000 acres (4,500 hectares).

Oxford in 1900 still had echoes of Christminster in Thomas Hardy's *Jude the Obscure* when, on market days, flocks and herds obstructed the narrow medieval streets and carriers' waggons clustered about the church of St Mary Magdalen. The city largely depended for its prosperity on its traditional role as a provider of goods and services to the university and the surrounding countryside, and Oxford's Victorian suburbs, dismissed by Gerard Manley Hopkins as 'a base and brickish skirt', provided a welcome additional source of consumers. A commentator in 1907 remarked that Oxford seemed destined never to have a major industry and, if it was untrue that the city's only manufactures were parsons and sausages, its major employers were Oxford University Press, the railways, the building trade and local breweries. Both men and women were employed in college service and women found work in three clothing factories, local shops and domestic service. Irregular employment caused financial problems for many Oxford households, particularly during the university's long vacation when college servants were out of work, trade was slack and, according to tradition, grass grew in the High Street. The development of the motor industry transformed the city within a generation, providing work on such a scale that it not only cured underemployment in Oxford and district but also drew in thousands of people from further afield.

The process of Oxford's expansion in the twentieth century was determined by a number of factors. Chance clearly played a part since, as Thomas Sharp pointed out in 1948, the motor industry was only based in Oxford because William Morris had started a workshop in his parents' back garden. Perhaps also, if the old Oxford Military College buildings had not been available in 1912, Morris might have chosen somewhere other than Cowley to locate his first factory. In some ways his choice of site was inspired since, given the geography of Oxford, the development of the works and associated housing estates did little to impinge upon the historic city. The flood plains of the Thames and Cherwell provided a physical barrier between old and new Oxford and members of the university and North Oxford residents had always tended to look upon the area east of Magdalen Bridge as being part of another world. Development land was therefore cheaper and easier

A pedestrian prepares to dash between vehicles in a busy High Street, May 1935.

to obtain but the dizzying pace of growth between the wars inevitably raised fears that Oxford was going to become a huge industrial sprawl. The Oxford Preservation Trust was founded in 1926 to safeguard the green setting of the city and its strategic purchases of land have helped to save many crucial areas from development. The first Oxford town planning map was produced in 1928 and the planning process began to have an effect in determining the future shape of the city.

The motor industry brought prosperity to the city but Oxford has always struggled to adapt to its products. Situated at the junction of two major routes, the A40 running east–west and the A34 running north–south, Oxford soon found its main streets filled with local and long-distance traffic and the first part of the city's ring road was opened in 1932. The topography of the city, funnelling traffic into a bottleneck at Magdalen Bridge, encouraged Lawrence Dale to suggest a relief road across Christ Church Meadow in 1940 and this proposal later became official policy, exciting huge controversy and passionate debate before it was eventually scrapped in 1966. A later relief road, the so-called Eastwyke Farm road, was dropped by the City Council in 1972 and several schemes to bypass Botley Road have come to nothing. The Oxford ring road was eventually completed in 1966 and two river crossings, Donnington Bridge in 1962 and Marston Ferry Road in 1971, have assisted the movement of local traffic. The City introduced its *Balanced Transport Policy* in 1973 in order to limit traffic growth in the city centre and improve conditions for cyclists and pedestrians. Park and ride buses, bus lanes and cycle lanes soon became an established feature of Oxford and the *Oxford Transport Strategy*, devised by Oxford City Council and Oxfordshire County Council, went a step further in 1999 by introducing partial pedestrianisation in the city centre. The outcome of this major change continues to inspire spirited argument.

Largely spared by road builders and unscathed by wartime bombing, the centre of Oxford was nevertheless much adapted during the twentieth century. Expansion of the university and colleges was responsible for many changes and prominent additions include the New Bodleian Library in Broad Street, Nuffield College, the Sacher Building of New College and the University Science Area. Commercial development has radically altered the main shopping streets, generally replacing small shops with larger units but, in the case of the Clarendon Centre in 1985, going some way towards reversing that trend. Slum clearance before and after the Second World War has almost completely obliterated the old areas of St Aldate's and St Ebbe's and recast them as a modern adjunct to the city. By contrast, many major Oxford buildings have been thoroughly restored since the 1950s, banishing forever that air of picturesque and soot-stained decay for which Oxford was once well known. At the same time, the surviving town houses of Oxford have become more highly prized and the humble façades of Trinity Cottages in Broad Street were, for example, retained in 1969. Now, even the showy late Victorian and Edwardian frontages of Elliston's department store are preserved in the current Debenham's development in Magdalen Street.

While the motor industry continued to grow remorselessly, a *Punch* cartoon in 1936 showed Oxford dons filling their mortar boards with money from Lord Nuffield's (motor) horn of plenty. Oxford seemed destined to become a purely industrial city, the Motopolis of John Betjeman's *Oxford University Chest*, and the university to become simply 'the Latin Quarter of Cowley'. Postwar planning stemmed the growth of Oxford, however, and factories at Swindon, Swansea, Theale and Linwood met the increasing demand for Morris and Pressed Steel products. Since the 1950s, the vicissitudes of the British motor industry have made it an unlikely benefactor and the Cowley workforce shrank from a peak of 28,000 to about 6,000 in 1999. The demolition of the North and South Works, the old Morris Motor factories, in 1993, was symptomatic of an industry struggling to reshape itself for the future. Academic Oxford has, by contrast, burgeoned since the war with the help of both public and private funds. Oxford University today has 17,000 students, up from 7,200 in 1950, and almost every college has expanded its numbers; eight new colleges have been founded or achieved fully chartered status since 1960. Current and proposed developments include the Said Business School near the railway station and an Islamic Centre in Marston Road. In 1993, the city acquired a second thriving university when Oxford Polytechnic became Oxford Brookes University and this now has nearly 15,000 students. As traditional manufacturing has shrunk, academe has re-established itself and has helped to attract to the city a range of high technology and scientific industries. At the same time, the recent growth of supermarkets, restaurants and bars in and around Oxford has restored the old importance of goods and services in the local economy.

Every place has its characters but Oxford has more than most because it is both a local community and a university city with national and international links. Since 1914, no fewer than nine British prime ministers, including Margaret Thatcher and Tony Blair, have been educated at Oxford and Bill Clinton, former President of the United States, was a Rhodes Scholar at Oxford in 1968–70; Indira Gandhi, Benazir Bhutto and Imran Khan were all educated there. Thanks to the work of Howard Florey and his colleagues at the Sir William Dunn School of Pathology, penicillin was clinically tested for the first time in Oxford in 1941. J.R.R. Tolkien and C.S. Lewis were Oxford dons whose books are universally known. Such connections give a wider dimension to many Oxford issues and they are, of course, a blessing

to local journalists, providing an Oxford angle on many world events. Any list of truly local characters of the century must include T.E. Lawrence (Lawrence of Arabia); the Liberal MP, Frank Gray, and his one-time friend William Morris, Lord Nuffield; and Olive Gibbs, born in St Thomas's, who was a doughty campaigner on many issues. The photographs in this book illustrate many other local people who have coloured, enriched and even saved the lives of others.

Fred Ingram (left) and Olive Gibbs (second from right) lead a Campaign for Nuclear Disarmament march through Cornmarket Street, about 1960.

1915 Bullnose Morris car and convalescing soldiers outside the Masonic Buildings in High Street. The Masonic became part of the 3rd Southern General Hospital during the First World War but many older Oxonians will have happier memories of the building as a dance hall, The Forum.

The Start of the Century

May Day in Oxford in 1912 when a parade of brewery drays formed part of the annual celebration of spring. Then as now, crowds gathered on Magdalen Bridge on May morning to hear the choristers sing from Magdalen Tower at 6 a.m.

1900   Sheep roast at Headington Quarry in November. This event was held annually at the turn of the century to commemorate the dedication of the parish church, Holy Trinity. Half a ton of coal was needed to roast the sheep and children swarmed around the fire trying to get dripping from the spit on to bits of bread. The mutton was carved and eaten in the evening at the nearby Six Bells.

1901   The official ceremony at the University Church of St Mary the Virgin on 25 January, when Edward VII was proclaimed King following the death of Queen Victoria. Recalling age-old divisions between Town and Gown, civic leaders also announced the new reign at the foot of Carfax Tower, the last remnant of the City Church of St Martin demolished in 1896.

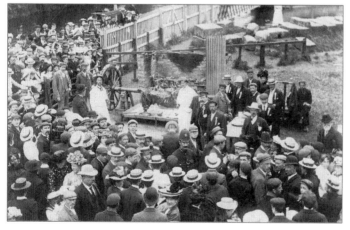

1902   Ox roast at Osney Lock to celebrate the coronation of Edward VII on 9 August. The victim, a Hereford heifer, had been given a brief reprieve when the King's illness caused a postponement of the coronation in June; now, in just three and a half hours, beginning at 9.30 a.m., the carcase was reduced to a skeleton.

1904 Watched by crowds in Radcliffe Square and by spectators from every available window, doorway and balcony, the Encaenia procession passes Brasenose College. On this occasion, the ceremony in the Sheldonian Theatre was to include the installation of the Chancellor, Viscount Goschen, the robed figure with two page boys, as well as the customary award of honorary degrees.

1905 The University College VIII at the college barge during Eights Week. The crew had a successful week, 'bumping' Christ Church and New College. The ornamental college barges, lining the river beside Christ Church Meadow, provided social and changing facilities and served as viewing platforms during the races.

1906 Self-portrait of T.E. Lawrence, the future Lawrence of Arabia (standing, right) while he was at the City of Oxford High School for Boys; he took the picture using a bicycle pump under his jacket linked by rubber tubing to the camera. A.W. Cave, headmaster of the school between 1888 and 1925, is seated in the centre of the group.

1906 A swimmer at Parsons' Pleasure looks understandably apprehensive as a naked man does a header off the diving board. Nude bathing remained a feature of this varsity bathing place on the river Cherwell until it was closed in 1992. To spare their blushes, ladies punting on the river were supposed to disembark and walk round to the other side of the bathing place.

1906 Children wearing hand-me-downs at Headington Quarry Church of England School. There was considerable poverty in Oxford's courts and yards and in the still rural villages on the fringes of the city. In Quarry, villagers struggled to make ends meet by taking in laundry from Oxford, and the hedgerows were formerly festooned with washing on dry days.

1906 Employees of the Oxfordshire Steam Ploughing Company, later John Allen & Son, at the firm's works in Hockmore Street, Cowley. This business, established in 1868, manufactured and hired out steam ploughing equipment and other machinery and introduced a significant industry to the village. In the 1920s, it was literally to pave the way for the motor industry by preparing the site for the new Cowley factories.

c. **1907** Hire cars outside William Morris's Holywell Street Garage; the proud proprietor is seated on the far right. Beginning as a cycle maker at the family home in James Street in 1893, Morris opened a central shop at no. 48a High Street in 1899 and took over the Holywell premises by 1902. He built a new and splendid garage on the site in 1910 and assembled his first Bullnose Morris there in 1912.

1907 A crowded St Giles' Fair with St Mary Magdalen Church in the distance beyond the taximen's shelter and the helter-skelter. The former parish wake had become a major pleasure fair in Victorian times with special trains bringing in visitors from far afield. Here, dancers at Jacob Studt's Bioscope show are busy attracting customers to the novel excitement of moving pictures.

1907 High Street looking east from Carfax with pedestrians free to stand or wander in the road with impunity; on the left, two children are standing outside Gill & Co.'s old established ironmonger's shop. At this time, the local tramways company was battling unsuccessfully to introduce electric trams in place of the old horse trams seen further down the street.

1907 Cornmarket Street, looking north past the Clarendon Hotel. Shop blinds are down to keep the sun off the stock at Twining's high class grocery shop and, further down the street, at Morton's the draper's. The London & North Western Railway Company's office is visible beside the entrance to the Clarendon Hotel livery stables.

1908 Children with May garlands outside the village school in Iffley. This was a respectable revival of an old May Day custom which, to judge from exasperated remarks in Victorian school log books, had given children the chance to take a day off school and go begging round their villages.

1910 Class A at Temple Cowley School when neither teacher nor children noticed the misspelling. The identified pupils are, from left to right: back row, Lucy Pether, Ada King, Edna Smith, Nellie Alder, Mabel Saker and three girls from Cowley barracks; middle row, -?-, Jim Brandish, -?-, -?-, -?-, Harry Pullin, -?-, -?-, -?-; front row, -?-, -?-, -?-, Bill Davies, Bill Allison, Elsie Davies, Sybil Thomas, Olive Aldridge, two girls from the barracks. The sheepdog, Rebecca, belonged to the Revd George Moore, the controversial vicar of Cowley from 1875 to 1928.

c. **1910** A brave cyclist squelches into the road to demonstrate the appalling mud in Crescent Road in Cowley. Conditions like this would have been banished from Oxford's roads by this date but Cowley remained outside the City boundary until 1929.

1909 Children peer between the horses as the Bees, members of the University College second cricket eleven, prepare to leave by coach for a match at Wallingford; to judge from the coats and the wet road surface, it was hardly cricketing weather. The Edwardian years were marked by nostalgia for the old days of coaching and the Blenheim coach was regularly used and photographed in and around Oxford.

1908 Still smart survivors of the Gridiron Club Ball are photographed in the early morning outside the Town Hall. Such balls were quite formal occasions with chaperones in attendance and dance cards upon which the ladies recorded the names of their intended dancing partners; nevertheless, there seems to have been some scope for flirtation.

1909 Commemoration Week at the end of Trinity Term brought a sudden feminine influx to the predominantly male university. This photograph, taken in University College, shows undergraduates positively outshone by womenfolk wearing an array of remarkable hats.

1912 A parade of brewery drays, seen here at The Plain, was a feature of May Day in Oxford. Brewing was a traditional and important Oxford industry and Hall's Oxford Brewery Ltd had developed through mergers into a substantial business; the parade was, in fact, so large that Henry Taunt, the photographer, had to combine two photographs to create this image.

1913 Beaters of the parish boundaries gather with their willow wands on the steps of the Town Hall on Ascension Day; the veteran Oxford photographer, Henry Taunt, with yachting cap and white beard, is on the right in the back row. Beating the Bounds continues today and, by tradition, when the beaters reach Lincoln College, the boys scrabble in the quad for hot pennies thrown from the windows.

c. **1913** The manager and staff photographed outside the Electra Palace cinema in Queen Street. Permanent cinemas soon made an appearance to meet public demand for the movies and the Electra, central Oxford's first purpose-built cinema, opened on 25 March 1911. In order to limit varsity rowdyism during performances, the management made undergraduates pay one shilling for admission.

1913   An up-to-date Daimler bus stands at the Magdalen Road terminus, drawing attention away from the out-of-date horse tram. Disgusted by delays in providing Oxford with modern public transport, William Morris and his friend Frank Gray, a local solicitor, worked together to introduce a rival motor bus service from 5 December 1913. The tramway company admitted defeat in January 1914, abandoned their horse trams and took over Morris's buses.

1912   The scene at Carfax on 13 September as a huge procession heads towards the railway station with the coffins of two airmen from the Royal Flying Corps who had been killed in a plane crash at Wolvercote three days before. This was one of the world's first military aircraft fatalities and it caused a local sensation; 2,226 people subscribed to a plaque that was subsequently put up near the scene of the crash in Godstow Road.

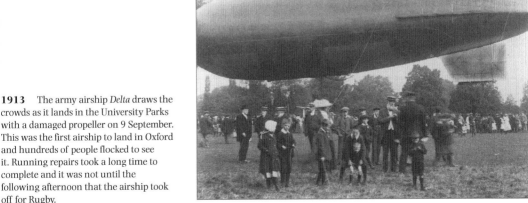

1913   The army airship *Delta* draws the crowds as it lands in the University Parks with a damaged propeller on 9 September. This was the first airship to land in Oxford and hundreds of people flocked to see it. Running repairs took a long time to complete and it was not until the following afternoon that the airship took off for Rugby.

1913 Members of Oxford University's Officer Training Corps Army Signal Service Units who took on their Cambridge equivalents. This photograph is from an album kept by Corporal John Mackreth (back row, centre) who joined the Royal Engineers when war broke out and died in France on 5 September 1916.

1914 The Oxford City police force often had problems in dealing with over-exuberant undergraduates but, in this view taken at the Commem Ball in June, there is a rare moment of truce. Within a matter of weeks, the youthful high spirits of Oxford were to be put into perspective by the outbreak of the First World War.

The First World War

Tented hospital in New College garden during the First World War when many of Oxford's public buildings became temporary hospitals to cope with the flood of casualties from the Western Front.

1914   The recruiting sergeant encourages men to join the army at St Giles' Fair. Whether motivated by patriotism or embarrassed by 'white feather' campaigns against apparent cowards, men joined the forces in huge numbers and conscription only became necessary in 1916.

1914   Many Belgian refugees flooded into the country at the outbreak of the war and were generally well received. Some refugees, including the Van Russin family illustrated here, found their way to Oxford and they were initially accommodated at Ruskin Hall, the working men's college established in 1899.

c. **1914** The Oxford Volunteers parade on Balliol College cricket field. They were an early home guard, comprising the old, the middle-aged and those whom the recruiting officers had rejected; in the university they were known affectionately as Godley's Own Oxford Volunteers after their Colonel, A.D. Godley. The group includes the Poet Laureate, Robert Bridges (third from right) and Sir Walter Raleigh, Professor of English Literature (second from right).

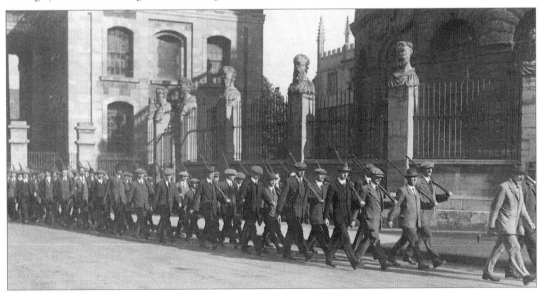

c. **1914** Godley's volunteers march past the Sheldonian Theatre, probably on their way back from manoeuvres in the University Parks. On one such occasion, Sir Walter Raleigh went straight into the Clarendon Building on Delegates' business 'cold, dirty, dishevelled but happy' that he had found himself a small part in the war that his sons were fighting.

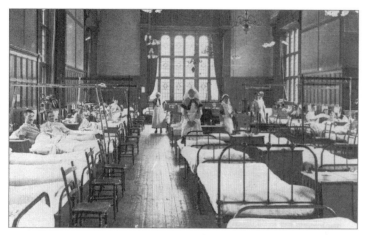

c. **1915** Surgical Ward 7 in one of the Writing Rooms at the Examination Schools. The 3rd Southern General Hospital was established in Oxford in August 1914 and the Examination Schools were requisitioned as the hospital headquarters. As the numbers of casualties at the front multiplied, troop trains brought in thousands of wounded men and the airy building became filled with beds and patients; temporary huts occupied the courtyard.

c. **1915** Operating theatre in the Examination Schools. Many of the casualties arrived in need of further surgery and this picture shows masked and gowned surgeons with their assistants, apparently ready to operate on the next patient.

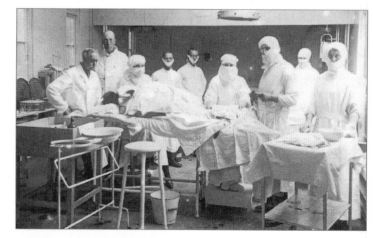

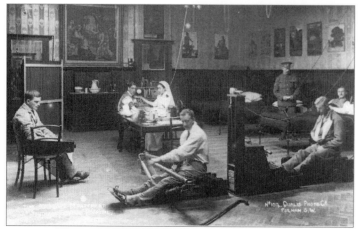

c. **1915** Medical facilities included a massage department where a nurse appears to be administering electro-massage to a patient with a machine plugged into a light socket. A rowing machine and other equipment provided physiotherapy for other convalescents.

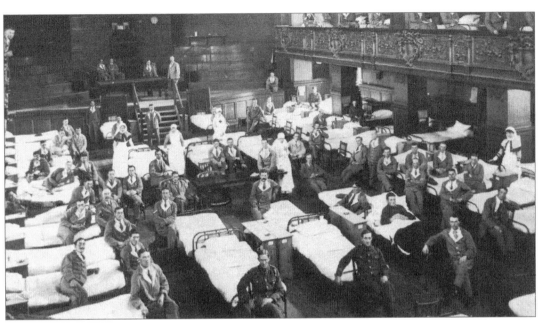

c. **1915**   The main hall in the Town Hall also became part of the hospital in October 1914 and beds filled both the auditorium and the balconies. The stage at the far end seems to have been left clear for patients who were becoming mobile again.

c. **1915**   Tented hospitals were created in several college gardens and New College garden must have provided a gloriously peaceful location for these patients, offering a striking contrast with the horrors of the trenches from which they had come.

c. **1915** The inmates of Oxford workhouse in Cowley Road were evacuated and the premises became the Cowley Section of the 3rd General Hospital for the duration of the war. The photograph shows recuperating soldiers outside the main entrance to the building.

c. **1915** As the men recuperated and needed something to do, carpentry and boot repairing workshops were laid on for those from suitable backgrounds; this boot workshop at Cowley includes two identified men, Wilson (fifth from left) and Morison (third from right). Volunteers also provided sewing materials so that men could while away the hours embroidering their regimental crests.

1917 Young men were not all so easily occupied, however, and the City authorities became concerned about the number of women attracted into Oxford by the prospect of a good time with the convalescing soldiers. In March, Miss G. Costain became the first woman police constable appointed to the Oxford City force, and 'stirred things up a bit amongst the "flappers"'.

c. **1915**   There are few records of the hundreds of doctors, nurses and orderlies who worked in the 3rd Southern General Hospital but Sister Grundy, photographed outside the nurses' quarters at Merton College, was clearly somebody's heroine and her cheerful smile must have lit up many wards.

***c.* 1916** Munitions workers at the Oxfordshire Steam Ploughing Company in Cowley, which was turning out more than 1,000 Stokes bomb cases a week.

1916 A week's output of Bullnose Morris cars stands outside the Hollow Way factory. William Morris had acquired the former Oxford Military College buildings in 1912 and production of the Bullnose Morris began here in March 1913. The firm, known as WRM Motors Ltd from 1912, continued to make cars during the war but it largely concentrated on war production.

c. **1917** A Bullnose Morris converted for use as a light armoured car takes part in a procession along High Street during Feed the Guns Week.

c. 1916 Women munitions workers taking over from the men at WRM Motors Ltd. They have been identified as follows, from left to right: Win White, Flo White, Rose Titcombe, -?-. Morris's factory turned out hand grenades, Stokes bomb cases and mine sinkers in such quantities that a railway siding was built to link the factory with the nearby Great Western Railway line.

1917 Some men were retained as essential workers and there were enough of them to form a WRM Motors United football team in the 1917/18 season. W.R. Morris is standing at the back of the group on the left and the captain, Bill Anstey, is seated (centre) behind the football.

WOMEN WHO WILL WORK DURING THE WAR.

1915 The *Oxford Journal Illustrated* praises the spirit shown by women ticket collectors at the Great Western Railway station and by Miss Wiggins of Market Street who was delivering bread and flour because her brother was at the Front. The first Oxford postwomen began delivering mail in December 1915 and conductresses appeared on the Oxford buses in the early months of 1916.

1915 Oxford boy scouts collect money and materials for the war effort in High Street. Their efforts were probably a part of Red Cross Day on 5 June when street collections, an auction and a concert raised over £1,600.

1918 An aerial view of wartime allotments on Merton Field. All over Oxford land was taken over for food production as the U-boat menace forced the country to grow more food and reduce imports. The view also shows Merton College and the adjoining Fellows' Garden behind a surviving piece of the medieval city wall.

NURSE'S GREAT VICTORY SALE

To commemorate

The Glorious Allied Victory.

We have decided to allow those who are now serving, or who have already served, in H.M. Forces and their relatives, also those included in the following List, a Special Discount of 10 per cent. off all Furs purchased during the Next Four Weeks.

The Army.
The Navy.
Air Service.
Wireless Stations.
Munitions.
Volunteers.
Special Constabulary.
Police Force.
Fire Brigade.
Post Office.
Civil Service.
Agriculture.
Small Arms Manufacture.
Armament Works.
Aircraft Factories.
The Merchant Service.
Food Distributors.
The Various Control
Departments.

NURSE, Manufacturing Furrier,

OPPOSITE THE TOWN HALL.

1918 Relief and elation greeted the end of the war in November and there were lively scenes as the Kaiser's effigy was burned in St Giles' and red paint was daubed on some of the Emperors' heads outside the Sheldonian Theatre. Nurse's, manufacturing furriers in St Aldate's, launched an improbable Victory Sale offering a 10% discount to those who had served in the forces or otherwise assisted the war effort.

1919 The University pays tribute to the victorious Allies. The recipients of honorary degrees included, from left to right: back row, Henri Pirenne, Rear Admiral Sir William Hall, Rt. Hon. J.R. Clynes, Lord Robert Cecil; front row, Lieut. General Sir John Monash, General Pershing, General Joffre, Lord Curzon (Chancellor of the university), Field Marshal Sir Douglas Haig, Admiral Sir David Beatty, Herbert Hoover, Sir Henry Wilson.

Between the Wars

High Street traffic congestion in 1935. The rapid industrialisation of Oxford between
the wars and the growth of long-distance road traffic soon brought chaos to the city's
once-peaceful main streets. An experimental rubber road was laid in Cornmarket Street
and the first part of the city's bypass was built in 1932.

1920 Crowds of people completely block Carfax as Oxford comes to a halt during the two minutes' silence on the second anniversary of Armistice Day. Amidst the throng, a sandwich-board man advertises Nurse's furs.

1921 Homes for Heroes; part of the Oxford City Council housing estate in Cowley Road where ex-servicemen and their families were preferred as tenants. These houses were among the first to be built in Oxford following the Housing Act of 1919 and they were designed in a cottage style by the Oxford Panel of Architects; more than 2,000 council houses were built in the City between the wars.

1923 Men at work in the University Parks, constructing the High Bridge over the river Cherwell. Unemployment was a problem in the city immediately after the war and this was one of a number of public works designed to provide useful jobs. The bridge itself had a mixed reception, one wit remarking that its height was to enable a review of the Fleet on the Cherwell.

c. 1922 A sunny afternoon in Cornmarket Street with a Bullnose Morris heading south towards Carfax and shoppers still able to amble across the road without a care. On the right, W.H. Smith's is at no. 22 with Fuller's café at no. 24; the 'Wet Off' sign announces Zacharias & Co., suppliers of waterproof clothing near the Ship Street corner.

c. 1922 Eights Week in full swing as crowds in boats and on the banks of the river watch the racing and enjoy the sunshine. The New College 1st VIII rowed over on all six days and remained Head of the River; after the last race, excited New College undergraduates jumped into the river and swam out to greet the victorious crew.

1923 A Webber's delivery van stands in St Giles', ready for a procession of tableaux and decorated vehicles during the Oxford Shopping Carnival. The smart vehicle demonstrates the elegance of Webber's department store in High Street which boasted 'Millinery of Style and Distinction'. Oxford businesses flourished between the wars, benefiting from the growth of Oxford and local prosperity.

1923 Election card sent by Frank Gray, Oxford's populist Liberal MP, to the Monk family of Cherwell Street. Frank Gray, the unconventional son of a leading Oxford Conservative, Ald. Sir Walter Gray, took the Oxford constituency in November 1922 and held the seat in 1923 after bitter arguments about Free Trade with his former friend, William R. Morris. He seemed destined for political success but he was later unseated because he had inadvertently exceeded his election expenses.

c. **1921** Expansion begins at Cowley as the Morris factories outgrow the original Hollow Way premises and extend along Garsington Road. Following Morris's bold price cut in 1921, car sales soared and production at the plant rose from 1,932 vehicles in 1920 to 58,436 in 1930. The development of the motor industry between the wars soon transformed Oxford into a large industrial city with full employment.

1927 The machine shop at Pressed Steel on 18 June. The Pressed Steel site at Cowley was developed from green fields to a large enterprise employing 1,100 people within a year; by 1939, the workforce was 5,250. The massive scale of the Morris and Pressed Steel businesses provided work throughout the Oxford region and attracted new residents from Wales and other depressed areas.

c. **1928** MG 'M' type Midgets outside the Edmund Road factory. The letters MG stand for Morris Garages and the first MG special was assembled in the Longwall Street garage in 1924. Demand for the cars became so great that this factory in Cowley, the first special-purpose sports car factory in the world, was built in 1927. It was soon outgrown, however, and MG production moved to Abingdon in 1929.

1927 Edward, Prince of Wales, the future Edward VIII, visits the Morris Motors factory. Leaning nonchalantly on his stick, he is seen here talking to Edward Brooks, a Headington man who had won the Victoria Cross as a Company Sergeant Major during the War.

c. **1929**   F. Cape & Co., drapers in St Ebbe's Street, hire
a donkey to provide an original sale advertisement. Cape's
adapted their main shop to the changing times by creating a
walk-in arcade in the 1930s to attract window shoppers into
their premises.

1930   Hollywood film star Tallulah Bankhead at the
Oxford gasworks. The launch of a balloon brought her to
these unlikely surroundings where she kissed the intrepid
fliers from the Oxford University Balloon Union before
they ascended.

c. **1930** Squalid conditions for slum dwellers in Carter's Yard, St Aldate's. Just a few steps away in Christ Church, gilded Oxford youths such as Sebastian Flyte in Evelyn Waugh's *Brideshead Revisited* were living a rather different life, feasting on plovers' eggs and lobster Newburg and sipping Cointreau on their balconies.

1931 The Duchess of York, later the Queen Mother, opens the Radcliffe Maternity Home in Walton Street on 22 October. She is accompanied, on her right, by the future Lord Nuffield who funded this development and poured huge sums of money into medical research; in 1937 he founded Nuffield College, although building was delayed until after the Second World War.

c. **1933**   A family outing along the southern bypass.
The southern bypass between Hinksey Hill and Botley was
built in 1932 and formed the first part of the Oxford ring
road; it was known mockingly as 'The road from nowhere
to nowhere'. The completion of the northern bypass
between Headington and Eynsham in 1935 had much more
effect in diverting traffic away from the city centre.

c. **1934**   The Oxford Super Cinema in Magdalen Street,
photographed about ten years after its opening in 1924.
Designed by J.C. Leed, the cinema provided seats for 1,300
people. The first 'talkie' screened in Oxford was shown at the
Super in January 1930 and, in September 1940, this was
the first Oxford cinema to open on Sundays.

1935 Cornmarket Street decorated for the Silver Jubilee. F.W. Woolworth's 3*d* and 6*d* store and H. Samuel's shop occupied the site of the city's old Roebuck Hotel, part of a growing trend which saw national and international businesses making an appearance in local high streets.

1935 A policeman sets out to clear the chaos in High Street during the Silver Jubilee celebrations. Motor vehicles, so crucial to the prosperity of Oxford, began to threaten the historic fabric of the city as traffic levels increased. At the junction of important east–west and north–south roads, the A40 and the A34, central Oxford became notorious for traffic jams.

1935 Orchard Street, St Ebbe's tea party in June when Oxford people extensively celebrated King George V's Silver Jubilee. Street parties were held in many areas, the city was decorated with flags and bunting and major public buildings were floodlit.

1936 The cycle race at the Oxford City Police Sports' Day in Iffley Road. This event involved constables in full uniform racing the bikes that they rode in more purposeful fashion while on duty; PC Shapland, on the inside, seems to be coming through strongly at this point in the race.

1937 Workmen install an experimental rubber road in Cornmarket Street. Fears that vibration caused by traffic would literally destroy Oxford's historic buildings led to the idea of providing a cushioned road surface. The rubber road was to have been extended into High Street, but motorists skidded helplessly when the surface was wet and the blocks were eventually removed in 1953.

1937 Crowds in Broad Street welcome Queen Mary on 25 June when she came to Oxford to lay the foundation stone of the new Bodleian Library. This massive building, designed by Sir Giles Gilbert Scott, was to provide staff accommodation, teaching rooms and eleven decks of stacks to relieve pressure on the overcrowded Bodleian Library.

1936 A 'flying' bike for just 75 shillings is the main attraction in this Oxford & District Co-op window display, probably at the Society's main store in George Street. Like the more expensive CWS cycles costing up to £6 7s 6d, this model promised reliability, easy running and the ability to overcome all obstacles.

1938 Council workmen erect a temporary gate before rebuilding the Cutteslowe Walls. The Cutteslowe council estate, seen in the background, was built in the early 1930s to rehouse families from central Oxford. In 1934–5, developers built private houses between the estate and Banbury Road and erected high brick walls across the roads to keep the council tenants out. The City Council had these walls demolished in 1938 but had to rebuild them after legal action.

1938 War seemed increasingly likely in the late 1930s and Starling's shop window display after the Munich crisis expressed the general sense of relief that the war clouds had passed. Never slow to miss a commercial opportunity, the Castle Street shop suggested that now was the perfect time to invest in a new carpet.

1939 William R. Morris, raised to the peerage in 1934 as Lord Nuffield, celebrates the completion of the millionth Morris, a Morris 14. He purchased the car himself and gave it to Guy's Hospital where it raised £1,700 as a prize in the hospital's appeal fund. By 1939, the Cowley factories were employing nearly 10,000 people.

1939 Oxford's country bus station in Gloucester Green. The growth of bus services in the 1920s led to the building of a bus station in Castle Street in 1929 but this soon became inadequate and congested. A new bus station was opened in Gloucester Green in 1935 following the removal of the cattle market to the Oxpens; the former Central Boys' School became a waiting room and offices and the dealers' settling room became a café.

The Second World War

Home Guards train on the Jackdaw Lane assault course in about 1943.
The Second World War brought huge numbers of evacuees to Oxford and the
city's industries moved swiftly into war production. Air raids seemed almost certain,
but Oxford was spared.

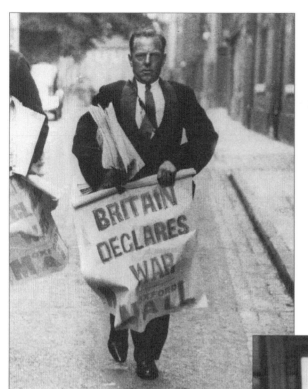

1939   A newsvendor hastens from Newspaper House in New Inn Hall Street with the special Sunday edition of the *Oxford Mail* that announced the outbreak of war on 3 September. The Prime Minister, Neville Chamberlain, broadcast the news at 11.15 a.m. and many local people would have heard his message on the wireless at home; his words were relayed to worshippers at St Giles' Church during the morning service.

1939   An evacuee, with his gas mask in a cardboard box, leads his sister out of Oxford station. Many evacuees were taken on by bus to their final destination but one such journey ended very quickly as the bus became wedged under the Botley Road railway bridge.

1939 Watched by a fascinated crowd of local children, Corporation workmen build a public air raid shelter in Windmill Road, Headington, in September. War brought new dangers and restrictions but, for many children, life almost began to resemble the movies. Troop movements were exciting and, if Canadian or American servicemen appeared, there was always a chance of going home with sweets, biscuits and other prized commodities.

1939 An Oxford policeman, setting an example by wearing his gas mask, gives directions to a passer-by in Queen Street. On the right, a sandwich board man advertises blackout materials from Starling's nearby premises in Castle Street.

1939 Women clerks emerge from a staircase at St John's College. Their 'invasion' of a masculine world was part of the relocation of several government departments to the comparative safety of Oxford; the Director of Fish Supplies from the Board of Trade occupied St John's, causing Oxford to be improbably described as 'the centre of the fishing industry'.

1940 Sir William Beveridge, Master of University College (standing left), offers a welcome to refugees from the London Blitz who were given temporary billets in the college in September. It was estimated that Oxford's population rose by between 10,000 and 15,000 during the month as official and unofficial evacuees flooded into the city.

1939 'The Rabbit', a prototype built at John Allen's. This remote-controlled tracked vehicle was designed for use against the German defences and, if successful, it might have realised the hopes of the contemporary song, 'We're Going to Hang out the Washing on the Siegfried Line'. The German blitzkrieg in May 1940, culminating in the Dunkirk evacuation, made further development unnecessary.

c. 1940 Members of the Home Guard platoon from John Allen & Son's Cowley factory prepare for rifle-shooting practice in a gravel pit at Burcot near Dorchester. Formed as the Local Defence Volunteers in May 1940, the Home Guard included men up to the age of sixty-five. The first item of uniform to be issued was an LDV armband and wits argued that the letters stood for 'Look, Duck and Vanish' or 'Long Dentured Veterans'.

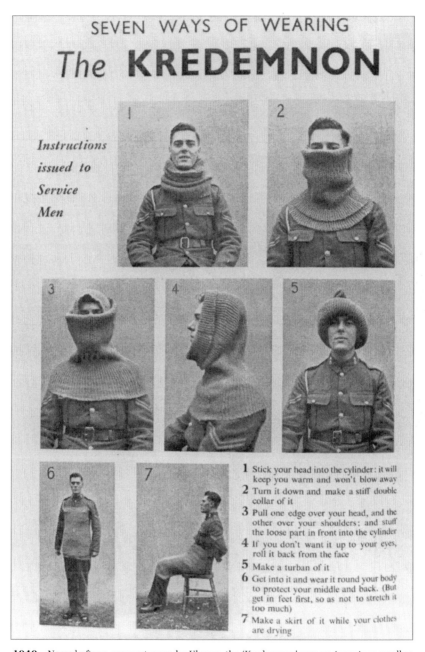

SEVEN WAYS OF WEARING
The KREDEMNON

Instructions issued to Service Men

1. Stick your head into the cylinder: it will keep you warm and won't blow away
2. Turn it down and make a stiff double collar of it
3. Pull one edge over your head, and the other over your shoulders; and stuff the loose part in front into the cylinder
4. If you don't want it up to your eyes, roll it back from the face
5. Make a turban of it
6. Get into it and wear it round your body to protect your middle and back. (But get in feet first, so as not to stretch it too much)
7. Make a skirt of it while your clothes are drying

1940 Named after a garment worn by Ulysses, the 'Kredemnon' was an ingenious woollen cylinder devised for servicemen by Mrs Marie Beazley, wife of the Lincoln Professor of Archaeology. She organised a team of 58 volunteers to knit Kredemnons and a knitting pattern with the more prosaic name 'The Greenock Multiwrap' encouraged the wider distribution of this Oxford invention.

c. 1940 Lord and Lady Nuffield lend their support to Alexandra Rose Day collectors who were about to enter the Morris Motors factories on the other side of Hollow Way. Lord Nuffield's modest office was on the top floor of this building, part of the former Oxford Military College, and it remained unchanged until the 1990s; elements of it may now be seen at the British Motor Industry Heritage Centre.

1940 The Spitfire 'City of Oxford' purchased for the Royal Air Force with money raised by the City of Oxford Fighter Fund. Later in the war, in 1943, the City adopted HMS *Enterprise* and the local press announced proudly that the vessel was involved in shelling the shore batteries at Cherbourg in June 1944; the ship's bell is now in the Town Hall.

c. **1940**   An ARP ambulance driver in gas mask and full gas-proof clothing peers out of her vehicle at the Norham Mews depot. The City Council established two wartime ambulance depots, this one in North Oxford and another in Cowley Place; the latter site was chosen because it would be able to serve the eastern half of the city if Magdalen Bridge was bombed.

1941 Firefighters demonstrate the new National Fire Service fire float, *Abel*, on the River Thames below the New Cut. This handsome craft, designed by Alexander Bell, the Divisional Fire Officer, saw no enemy action in a city that was fortunate enough to avoid air raids. In the distance, three pre-war boathouses are visible beside some of the remaining college barges.

c. **1941** The Mayor and the Vice-Chancellor launch a National Savings Week at Carfax; they are standing in front of a blast wall erected to provide protection for shoppers in the event of an air raid. Communities were given financial targets for these special weeks and Oxford, boosted by large personal donations from Lord Nuffield, comfortably exceeded them, encouraging rather smug comparisons with Cambridge.

69

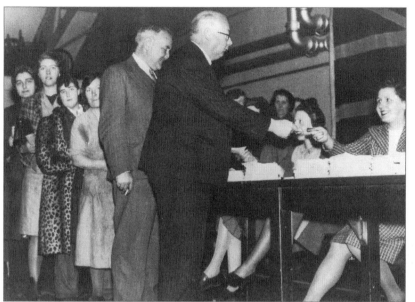

1941 Two of the managing directors at Morris Motors, H. Seaward and H.W. Ryder, reach the front of the queue for new points cards. Ministry of Food officials had made special arrangements to issue the cards during the lunch hour in the employees' canteen. The points system was a refinement of rationing, giving people a number of points each month and allowing them to buy certain commodities at any shop, not just at their registered supplier.

1941 Children and helpers outside Jesus College pavilion. The increasing number of women at work created a new demand for child-care facilities and day nursery places were provided for 500 children in Oxford by the end of 1943. Some day nurseries were in converted buildings like this pavilion, others were in purpose-built prefabricated structures.

c. 1941 Women operating small presses at Pressed Steel. The number of women working at the Pressed Steel factory soared from only 218 in 1938 to 2,435 in 1942 and more women than men were employed in the cartridge case factory built on the site in 1941.

1942 Employees from the Morris Motors factory in Cowley watch a tank demonstration by members of the Scots Guards Armoured Division 'somewhere on Salisbury Plain' on 27 October. During the war, Cowley produced more than 650 tanks.

1942 Wartime slogans, urging householders to 'Save Coal with Every Meal' and to 'Learn Just Where to Poke the Fire' welcome visitors to an Oxford Fuel Saving Exhibition. Another message, familiar to all who lived through the war years, exhorts people to 'Take a Weekly Bath not a Daily Bath and in not more than 5 inches of water'.

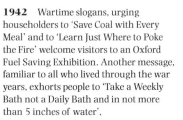

1943 Bren gun carriers on Exercise Spartan pass the Ashmolean Museum in March. Much of the action in this major training exercise took place in the Oxford area where British and Canadian forces advancing from 'Southland' met troops of Eastern Command representing a German 'Eastland'.

1944 Major John Howard, a former Oxford City policeman, leads the 2nd Battalion, Oxfordshire and Buckinghamshire Light Infantry, past the saluting base in St Giles' during Salute the Soldier Week. A few weeks later, on D-Day, he was spearheading the Normandy invasion by leading a glider-borne task force to capture two crucial bridges at Ranville and Benouville.

c. 1943 Oxford Home Guards surmount one of the many devilish challenges on the Jackdaw Lane assault course that opened in 1942. Sergeant Bint, a member of the 'Highlands' Platoon in Oxford, viewed the place with surprising affection at the end of the war, recalling that it was both useful and pleasurable to negotiate 'the well-thought out scheme of obstacles'.

c. 1944 A North Oxford ARP (Air Raid Precautions) detachment in the garden of 'Gunfield', Norham Gardens. The identified individuals are, from left to right: back row, -?-, Helena Deneke, Professor de Zulueta, Lerney, Weddisome, Miss Jonson of Lady Margaret Hall; middle row, Miss Dixon, O.H.E. Baker, -?-, Margaret Skipworth, -?-, -?-, C.V. Butler, -?-; front row, Lorimer, Lattey, Mrs Sanby, Brown, Intwickle, -?-, Margaret Deneke.

***c.* 1944** With petrol rationing and limited public transport, 'Holidays at Home' were a wartime necessity. Here, members of the Oxford Amalgamated Engineering Union Branch No.1 make the most of the weather during a river outing on a Salter's steamer.

1945 VE-Day (Victory in Europe) excitement in Wilkins Road on the Sunnyside estate in Cowley in May. Ron Smith, living round the corner in Oliver Road, recalled that 'a well-adorned string of highly coloured garments were suspended from two opposite houses and captioned "Hitler's impregnable line". What the line contained is not for me to say – but I was unaware that ladies did actually prefer such gaily coloured articles of clothing.'

The Postwar Period

The final demolition of the Cutteslowe Walls in 1959. Rationing had ended and,
according to the Prime Minister, Harold Macmillan, 'You Have Never Had It So Good'.
The removal of this pre-war class barrier between private and council estates fitted in
with the modernising spirit of the time.

1946 Consternation at the official opening of the New Bodleian Library on 24 October when the ceremonial key given to King George VI breaks in the lock; while efforts are made to retrieve the situation, Queen Elizabeth, in a fashionable hat, looks back towards the waiting crowd. After a long few minutes, the door was opened from inside and the ceremony continued.

1947 A study in concentration at the switchboards in Oxford telephone exchange. This manual switchboard behind the Head Post Office in St Aldate's had been built in 1934 to cope with the growing demand for trunk calls; telephone subscribers could subsequently make long-distance calls on demand instead of having to book them in advance. A new telephone exchange was built in Speedwell Street in 1959.

c. **1948** The queue was part of life in wartime and in the years of austerity that followed. This photograph was taken outside Timms Stores, a toyshop on the corner of George Street and New Inn Hall Street. Were these people queuing for fireworks or is there some truth in the story that passers-by simply joined a queue in case there was something good at the end of it?

1948 After the war, the City Council commissioned the town planner, Thomas Sharp, to present his recommendations for replanning Oxford. His radical proposals aimed to preserve the best of the old city while making drastic changes elsewhere. This model shows his plan for the western part of the city centre between Speedwell Street and Beaumont Street; major new roads included the Christ Church Meadow Road first suggested by Lawrence Dale in 1941.

c. **1950** Oxford's former Great Western Railway station from Park End Street when the view was dominated by posters advertising state electricity, Macleans toothpaste and Bile Beans. Thomas Sharp envisaged a combined bus and railway station on the site but, like many other aspects of his plan, this idea withered on the vine.

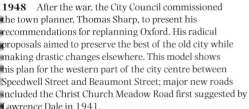

1950 Rush hour problems outside Pressed Steel as cyclists pour on to the Garsington Road at the end of a shift. After the war, the Cowley factories returned swiftly to peacetime production with a strong emphasis on the export market. Wartime camouflage on the factory buildings is still very evident.

c. **1952** A fleet of Prestcold 'Showmobiles' or mobile exhibition vehicles is launched at Cowley; the senior executives in attendance include, from left to right: W.G. Lambourn, F.E. Cairns, H.J. Wood, -?-, A.L. Shuttleworth, -?-, M.A.A. Bellhouse, -?-. These vehicles attended agricultural shows at home and abroad as Pressed Steel used its Prestcold subsidiary to exploit the postwar spread of commercial and domestic refrigeration.

1951 A little girl enjoys a snack among the crowds at St Giles' Fair. The Lady of the Lion Show attracts attention opposite the entrance to Little Clarendon Street, and Thurston's take the opportunity to advertise their smaller fair in the Cattle Market Paddock later in the week.

1951 B.R. Brown, the Pegasus goalkeeper wearing a large sticking plaster, helps to chair the captain after the team's 2–1 victory over Bishop Auckland in the FA Amateur Cup Final on 21 April. Pegasus was formed in 1948 and included players from both Oxford and Cambridge universities. It had an enormous local following and won the Amateur Cup again in 1952/53, beating Harwich and Parkeston 6–0 in the final.

1952 Watched by a large crowd, the Mayor's Sergeant, Leslie Boddy, leads the procession at Carfax after the proclamation of Queen Elizabeth II on 9 February. He is followed by Ald. King, Mayor of Oxford, W.J. Diplock, Recorder, Harry Plowman, Town Clerk, the Duke of Marlborough, Lord Sandford and the Chief Constable, C.R. Fox.

1953 Why are we waiting? A Welsh maid, Julia Snead (left) and the Bisto Kids, Ann (centre) and Susan Taylor, manage to look a little impatient before the coronation fancy dress parade in Mill Street. The terraced houses in the background are liberally festooned with celebratory flags and bunting.

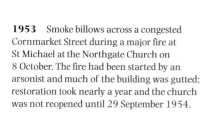

1953 Smoke billows across a congested Cornmarket Street during a major fire at St Michael at the Northgate Church on 8 October. The fire had been started by an arsonist and much of the building was gutted; restoration took nearly a year and the church was not reopened until 29 September 1954.

1953   Bags of swank as men of the Oxfordshire and Buckinghamshire Light Infantry march across Magdalen Bridge. The regiment was exercising, for the first time, privileges conferred when it was given the freedom of the city in 1948 and it marched through Oxford with band playing and colours flying. Crowds gathered to watch the event but the two women in the foreground seem to have had other things on their minds.

1954   Men forming the 22nd National Service intake arrive at Cowley Barracks, the regimental depot of the Oxfordshire and Buckinghamshire Light Infantry. The postwar Labour Government retained conscription in 1946 and National Service was only brought to an end in 1959.

1954 Albert Stewart from Jamaica, one of Oxford's first West Indian bus conductors, awaits passengers. Unable to match the wages paid to Cowley car workers and suffering from serious staff shortages, City of Oxford Motor Services Ltd appointed a number of black bus conductors, some of whom had only recently arrived in Britain.

1954 John Brookes, the Principal of the College of Technology, Art and Commerce, chats to the main prize-winners at the Old Catering Students' Association Dinner; they were, from left to right: Ruth Howlett, Susan Harris, Janet Murphy. The college went on to become Oxford Polytechnic in 1970 and is now Oxford Brookes University.

1954 Roger Bannister becomes the first man to run the mile in less than four minutes on 6 May. Paced by Chris Brasher and Chris Chataway, Bannister won the race in a world record time of 3 minutes 59.4 seconds. The race was one of the events at a meeting between Oxford University and the Amateur Athletics Association at the Iffley Road Running Ground.

1957 The mock funeral of David Paton, an undergraduate sent down in March. Keble College stressed that he was being punished for his whole record at Oxford and not for his part in burning the Dean's bedding during a riotous Bump Supper. Paton's friends were reviving an old varsity custom that involved bearers carrying a disciplined student's 'coffin' down to the station for a rousing send-off.

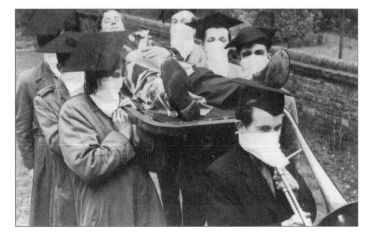

1954. Headington Quarry Morris Dancers outside the Chequers in the Quarry. William Kimber, seated in the centre of the group, was a member of the Quarry team in 1899 and helped Cecil Sharp to record many of their dances. The team in 1954 included, from left to right: back row, C. Jones, J. Phillips, J. Morris, J. Wardrop(?), R. Turrell, R. Phillips, A. Skyrme, F. Warland; middle row, K. Scivyer, F. Parsons, P. Scudder; front row, A. Kimber, J. Hutson.

1956 Women's work at the Jericho wharf on the Oxford Canal. Rosa Skinner (left) shovels coal from a narrow boat into the wheelbarrow steadied by Jean Humphries. Commercial traffic on the Oxford Canal had declined substantially and campaigners had beaten off an attempt to abandon the waterway in 1954.

1958 Some of the first residents on the Blackbird Leys estate. Oxford City Council approved the building of this new estate in 1957, partly to rehouse families who would be affected by the clearance of St Ebbe's. Blackbird Leys was named after a pre-existing farm on the site and housed about 7,000 people by 1965.

1959 Hugh Gaitskell, leader of the Labour Party, opens new premises for the New College Boys' Club on the Northway Estate. Youth clubs run by undergraduates dated from Victorian times and they were still very much needed in parts of Oxford with few recreational facilities. The Balliol Boys' Club was active in St Ebbe's and Worcester College Boys' Club in St Clement's.

1959 Leslie Davies fits the bonnet to a Morris Minor during the first night shift at the Cowley assembly plant. The Morris Minor, famously dismissed by Lord Nuffield as looking like a poached egg, was one of Cowley's postwar successes, introduced in 1948. Morris Motors Ltd merged with the Austin Motor Co. in 1952 to form the British Motor Corporation which accounted for 38.9% of domestic car production in 1955.

1959 Pathé News films J. Mitty, manager of the Oxfam shop at no.17 Broad Street. Oxfam, the Oxford Committee for Famine Relief, was founded in Oxford in 1942 and the Broad Street shop was its first retail outlet, opened by Cllr Kathleen Lower on 12 November 1947. The Pathé feature was looking into Oxfam's work for refugees.

1959 Council workmen demolish one of the Cutteslowe Walls between Wolsey Road and Carlton Road on 9 March. Those attending and enjoying the last act in this long saga were, from left to right, Mrs Williams, Ald. Marcus Lower, Ald. Mrs. Kathleen Lower, Cllr Mrs. Olive Gibbs and Cllr Edmund Gibbs.

1959 Cheerful youngsters occupy the diving boards at Tumbling Bay bathing place during the long hot summer. The City Council maintained four river bathing places that offered hours of free enjoyment to people who had little time or money for holidays. The cold water was perhaps less inviting for school swimming lessons in early May.

The 1960s and '70s

The Queen sees a model of the new Westgate Centre in 1968. 'Swinging' England was changing rapidly with huge house-building programmes, new roads and comprehensive redevelopment schemes; in Oxford, as elsewhere, there was some regret for what was being lost in the process.

1961 Polly the chestnut mare and her keeper, E. Bishop, do the South Oxford milk round for Mygdals' Dairies of Cumnor. The photograph was taken not because horse-drawn milk delivery was becoming a thing of the past but because Polly had nearly lost her life in deep mud only the day before.

1961 Gordon Varney, an inspection underforeman at Cowley, watches carefully as a Morris Mini-Minor body is lowered on to the sub-frame. Designed by Alec Issigonis, like the earlier Morris Minor, the Mini was introduced in 1959.

1961 The Mayor, Ald. Lionel Harrison, and Town Hall Keeper, Ernie Shenton, prepare to join a City Council outing on the Oxford Canal. Despite the mayor's informal garb, the excursion by narrow boat to Duke's Lock had a serious purpose; it was a feasibility study for Cllr Ferguson's suggestion that a relief road alongside the canal could solve Oxford's traffic problems.

1962 Ald. E.O. Roberts, Oxford's first Lord Mayor, takes full advantage of the new Donnington Bridge as his official car leads a procession of vehicles after the official opening on 22 October. Lord Hailsham, who had just opened the bridge, preferred to walk across, reflecting perhaps on his time at Oxford and his spell as the city's MP. The bridge provided a road link between south and east Oxford that had first been suggested in the 1920s.

1963 Emergency water supplies for the Walton Ale Stores; E. Vines delivers the day's water from a tank on a City Council lorry during the great freeze-up in February. Reg Eaton (left) was the grateful landlord.

1963 Members of the Oxford City Water Committee tour the Farmoor Reservoir construction site. This far-sighted scheme was the brainchild of Harold Crawley, the city's Water Engineer. The first reservoir, holding about 900 million gallons, was opened in 1962; Thames Water Authority completed the second stage reservoir, holding about 1,550 million gallons, in 1976.

1964   The Beatles, Ringo Starr, George Harrison, Paul McCartney and John Lennon, seen at the bar in Vincent's Club on 5 March. They came to Oxford in support of a campaign by Jeffrey Archer (half hidden by Paul) to raise £1 million for Oxfam.

1966   Mary Rand, the Olympic long jump gold medallist, takes a break during the opening of the Horspath Road Recreation Ground on 11 June. The new facilities included a pavilion, an athletics track, six soccer pitches, a hockey pitch and, in summer, two cricket pitches.

1966   Richard Burton and Liz Taylor arrive in Oxford to star in Marlowe's *Dr Faustus* at the Oxford Playhouse in February 1966. They are accompanied by Professor Nevill Coghill, who was producing the play and had persuaded them to come to Oxford. Richard Burton's connections with the city went back to 1944 when he undertook a short course at Exeter College.

1966 Oxford's oldest college servant, Dick Cadman, prepares to retire at the age of ninety-four. Known to generations of Trinity College undergraduates as Cadders, he had served the college for 67 years and, at the age of ninety-three, he was still getting up at 5.30 to begin the day's work on 'his' staircase.

1966 Jeanne Lindley uses a cooker as a practical example to teach a Pakistani woman the meaning of the verb, 'to open'. Many immigrants from the Indian sub-continent came to Oxford during the 1960s and the city also provided homes for Asians expelled from Uganda by President Idi Amin.

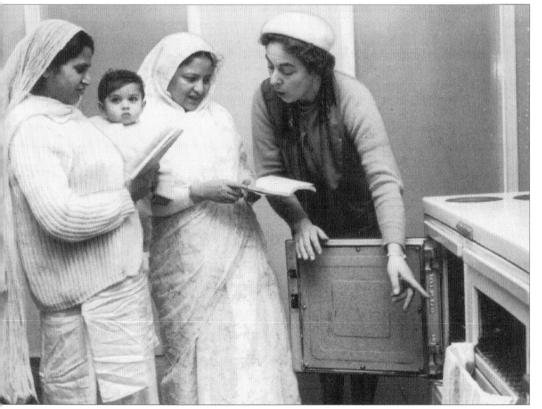

1967 'Relax by bus' becomes an unfortunate slogan as the Botley Road railway bridge claims another victim. For many years until the bridge was rebuilt in 1979, low double-deckers had to be used on Botley Road services and notices on other buses requested passengers to warn the driver if he or she seemed to be heading for the bridge.

1967 Pets and their owners assemble outside St Michael at the Northgate Church with the vicar, the Revd N. Macdonald Ramm. This was the church's second pets' service and included cats, dogs and Moses the tortoise, owned by Elizabeth Winning (third from left); Moses at least behaved very well during the service, sleeping from start to finish.

***c.* 1967** The Annual Church Parade of the Oxford City Police passes the reviewing platform in St Aldate's. A separate city police force ceased to exist in 1968 with the creation of the Thames Valley Police. Development on the corner of Speedwell Street and St Aldate's was soon to claim Raworth's, an old-established Oxford firm of coach builders that supplied W.R. Morris with car bodies in his early years at Cowley.

1968 Oxford United manager Arthur Turner hugs the captain, Ron Atkinson, after the team wins promotion to Division 2 by beating Southport 1–0. Known as Headington United until 1960, Oxford United secured a place in the Football League in 1962 and soon achieved fame by their giant-killing efforts in the FA Cup.

1968 Douglas Murray, the City Architect, shows Queen Elizabeth II and the Lord Mayor, Ald. Frank Pickstock, a model of the Westgate Shopping Centre during a royal visit to Oxford on 2 May.

1971 The last service held in All Saints' Church before the building was converted into a library for nearby Lincoln College. All Saints' was built in 1706–8 following the collapse of the medieval church in 1700 and it became the City Church in 1896 as a result of the closure and demolition of St Martin's, Carfax.

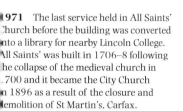

97

1971 Some of the staff of F. Cape & Co., the St Ebbe's Street drapers, gather behind the lingerie counter, just before the firm's closure. Cape's is still recalled fondly by older Oxford residents as the place where you could get anything and everything; until the 1960s, the shop had a cash railway which propelled your money across the ceiling to a central cash desk and shot your change back.

1972 J.R.R. Tolkien (left), having just been awarded a D.Litt. by the University, stands with the Vice-Chancellor, Sir Alan Bullock, on the steps of the Clarendon Building. Professor of Anglo-Saxon at Oxford from the 1930s and Merton Professor of English Language and Literature from 1945, Tolkien achieved international fame through his books, *The Hobbit* (1937) and *The Lord of the Rings* (1954–5).

1972 The sculptor Michael Black sees one of his newly carved Emperors' Heads lowered into place in front of the restored Sheldonian Theatre. The old heads, Victorian replacements for Wren's originals, had soon decayed and Max Beerbohm referred to 'their immemorial old age' in his novel *Zuleika Dobson* (1911). Some critics, including Nikolaus Pevsner, wanted to keep the eroded and weatherbeaten heads but the installation of new ones marked the completion of a major restoration project, one of many supported by the Oxford Historic Buildings Fund launched in 1957.

1972 Shoppers eye up the produce in Sainsbury's High Street store in 1972. The beautifully tiled walls and mosaic floors were standard and perhaps all Sainsbury's shops had the same enticing aroma? This was the firm's Oxford shop between 1911 and 1973 when Sainsbury's opened a new and, by comparison, enormous supermarket in the Westgate Shopping Centre.

1973 Oxford's first park and ride car park in Abingdon Road, opened in December. The facility was one outcome of the City's new *Balanced Transport Policy* which represented a huge shift away from grandiose road schemes towards measures designed to limit traffic in the historic city centre.

1974 The wives of some Cowley car workers march along Cowley Road, seeking to get their husbands back to work. Labour relations at the Austin-Morris plant were at a low ebb and stoppages at Cowley accounted for two-thirds of British Leyland's lost production in 1973. On this occasion, BL had sent all assembly plant workers home after a strike in the transport department. The wives' intervention excited huge media interest.

101

1976   Palm's delicatessen in Oxford Covered Market.
Mr and Mrs Palm came from Czechoslovakia to England
in 1938 and to Oxford a year later. They established their
delicatessen in 1954 when such shops were still quite rare
outside London and theirs was the first in Oxford to sell
such things as avocado pears, sweet potatoes and yams.
They retired in the early 1970s but the business still
flourishes.

1975   Employees at Oliver and Gurden's Bakery in Middle
Way, Summertown, pack Russian bars for Fullers Cakes.
Oliver and Gurden were two former chefs at Keble College
who established the Summertown Hygienic Steam Bakery
in 1919. They soon changed this name and Oliver and
Gurden's 'Famous Oxford Cakes' were a noted local product
until the closure of the bakery in December 1975.

1976   The Lord Mayor, Ann Spokes, puts in the first stitch as world champion letter writer, Raymond Cantwell, turns his hand to rug-making. Mr Cantwell was embarking on 202 hours of non-stop stitching to raise money for Age Action Year; other charities and Oxford hospitals benefited from his marathon sessions of ironing, playing darts, typing or letter writing.

1979   Farmers, dealers and stockmen gather in Oxford for the last time on 21 March. The last cattle auction at the Oxpens Cattle Market ended a link between Oxford and its rural hinterland that went back to the very beginnings of the city.

1979   Kumari Salgado, one of the 25 women who made history in the Michaelmas Term as the first female undergraduates at Lincoln College. John Grist, a gallant MA of the college, gave each of the women a houseplant to welcome them to the formerly male environment; one anonymous male student commented that the arrival of women had not affected sport at the college.

1979   The children's ward of the John Radcliffe Hospital which opened in Headington in October. The maternity hospital had already moved to the Headington site in 1972 and the new JR, as it was soon known, provided many of the services that had formerly been housed at the Radcliffe Infirmary in Woodstock Road. The contrast between this strikingly modern building and the old site could hardly have been more profound.

Modern Oxford

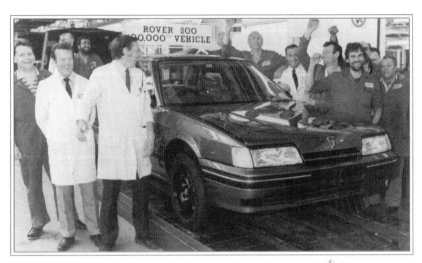

Employees at Cowley celebrate the 100,000th Rover 800 in 1988. BMW now owns
the Cowley car plant and Oxford has become part of the global economy but local issues
such as the university's refusal to give Mrs Thatcher an honorary doctorate, Bill Heine's
fibreglass shark and the Oxford Transport Strategy have continued to arouse
enormous passion.

1981 The Oxford crew and their cox, Sue Brown, experiment with rowing machines at the Swan Inn, Pangbourne, during training for the Boat Race. Sue Brown was the first woman to cox the Oxford boat in the Boat Race and she steered Oxford to victory by eight lengths.

1982 The Right Reverend Patrick Rodger, Bishop of Oxford, blesses Helen House, the world's first hospice for children. Mother Frances Dominica raised £500,000 in two years to build and furnish the hospice in the grounds of the All Saints' Convent in Leopold Street; it is named after Helen Worswick, a girl whom she had nursed.

1982 Shoppers browse among the market stalls at Gloucester Green. The open market had left Gloucester Green for the Oxpens in 1932 and its return seemed improbable as various plans were submitted for making more intensive use of the City-owned site. Following extensive public consultation, the City Council chose the so-called 'Romantic Option' for Gloucester Green in 1978 and the market came home in May 1982.

1982 The end of an era in Cornmarket Street as Woolworth's store, opened in 1957, gears up for its last Christmas. Woolworth's had wanted to build a new store on the site of the Clarendon Hotel in 1939 but the war and a battle to save the old building delayed the scheme. Finally, in 1954, Harold Macmillan, as Minister for Housing and Local Government, authorised plans designed by William, later Lord, Holford.

1983 'Go Home, Thatcher'; a demonstration by 500 students at Somerville when the Prime Minister, Margaret Thatcher, came to unveil a bust of herself at her old college. Two years later, Oxford University was again in the news when Congregation voted down proposals to give Mrs Thatcher an honorary degree.

1984 Elementary maths lesson at Barton Village First School as Steven Norris, MP for Oxford East, and Mrs Jane Foster-Jones, Secretary of Barton Schools Action Committee, remind children that 'Two Into One Doesn't Go'. The spirited campaign eventually defeated a proposed merger of local schools to save money.

1986   Robert Maxwell and team captain, Malcolm Shotton, triumphantly hold the Milk Cup trophy after Oxford United's 3–0 victory over Queen's Park Rangers. Maxwell was a hero for a time after rescuing the club from near bankruptcy in 1982 but he soon became a villain when he proposed a merger with United's local rivals, Reading, to create a team called Thames Valley Royals playing at Didcot.

1986   Four children enjoy the playground slide in modern St Ebbe's; they are, clockwise from top right, Olivia Graham, Peter Graham, Tom Azzopardi and David Azzopardi. Early 1960s council flats on the left began the redevelopment of St Ebbe's but, because of uncertainty over road schemes, much of the area remained blighted until the 1980s.

1986 Bill Heine poses with the fibreglass shark that had just been installed on the roof of his Headington home. This unusual townscape feature disconcerted City planners but it eventually won official blessing. Bill Heine added two other artworks to Oxford buildings, a pair of hands to his Penultimate Picture Palace and a showy pair of can-can dancer's legs to the Not the Moulin Rouge cinema.

1987 Fairgoers experience that sinking feeling while riding 'The Voyager' at St Giles' Fair. Despite the growth of theme parks with their white-knuckle rides, St Giles' Fair remains a popular annual event offering an ever-fascinating juxtaposition between fairground brashness and historic Oxford.

1987 Shoppers wander through one of the traffic-free and weatherproof malls of the Clarendon Centre. The new shopping centre, much criticised at first for the blue hoops fixed to Clarendon House, provided over 20 retail units on the site of Woolworth's store, Littlewood's and three shops in Queen Street. Older Oxonians regretted the loss of the disused Carfax Assembly Rooms, a popular venue for dances until the 1960s.

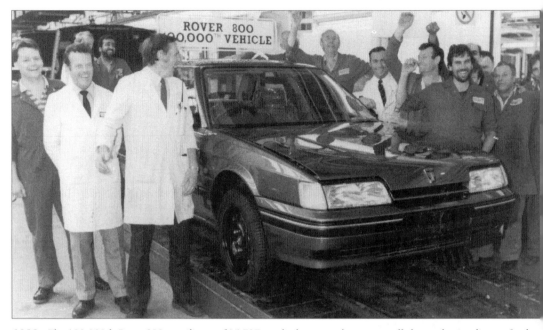

1988 The 100,000th Rover 800, retailing at £15,797 on the home market, comes off the production line at Cowley. Production of this model began in 1986 and, two years later, the factory was turning out 1,090 a week. BMW took over Rover in 1996 and its continued investment at the plant promises a twenty-first century future for an industry that began in an East Oxford back garden.

1991 Riot police stand outside the shops and flats in Blackbird Leys Road, sealing off an area known to joy-riders as The Manor. Blackbird Leys became the focus of unwelcome national attention in September when press and television were filled with pictures of joy-riding youths, burning cars and violent incidents. By October, road narrowing and the introduction of anti-skid surfaces had limited the opportunities for racing cars through the estate.

1989   Gary Mort and Richard Kemp, preceded by Mick Belson, ceremoniously remove a tall yucca plant from the building to mark the end of printing at Oxford University Press. They were taking the plant, nicknamed Bill Tin after a bonus scheme in which everything was built in, to the Kilner Ward of the Radcliffe Infirmary.

1991 Pickets from the National Union of Journalists outside Headington Hill Hall, headquarters of Robert Maxwell's Pergamon Press. For more than three years, between May 1989 and September 1992, this was the scene of a continuous picket following the company's sacking of 23 journalists for staging a 24-hour strike.

1991 Rogue Morris dancers provide an attraction for passing shoppers at Templars Square. By the 1980s, the open, windswept shopping malls of Cowley Centre were looking decidedly outmoded and unappealing. The modernisation of the shopping centre and the roofing of the malls transformed the place in 1989.

1992   Remembering the Inklings; Robin Isherwood: (left) unveils a plaque in the Eagle and Child pub in St Giles' to recall that C.S. Lewis, W.H. Lewis, J.R.R. Tolkien, Charles Williams and other literary figures met there regularly for beer and conversation on Tuesday mornings between 1939 and 1962. Their sessions at the 'Bird and Baby' could become quite lively and C.S. Lewis feared that other pub goers might have thought they were 'talking bawdy' when they were in fact discussing theology.

1993   Demolition contractors clear part of the North Works at Cowley. The British Leyland Motor Corporation became part of the Rover Group in 1986 and, in 1989, Rover decided to close the old Assembly Plant, preferring to concentrate production on the old Pressed Steel site east of the Eastern Bypass. The Oxford Business Park now occupies the vast Morris Motors site and skylarks nest in undeveloped corners.

1994   Andrew Smith, MP for Oxford East, cuts the ribbon to open Oxford Brookes University's third campus at Headington Hill Hall. Others present include, from left to right, Peter Bagnell, Chairman of Governors, Dr Clive Booth, the Vice-Chancellor and the Chancellor, Helena Kennedy QC. Robert Maxwell had installed the stained glass window in the background while he leased the building from Oxford City Council.

1995   Tish Francis, Hedda Beeby and Oxford Playhouse staff celebrate the news of a £2.5 million National Lottery award to refurbish the theatre. The Playhouse, built in Beaumont Street in 1938, was closed with financial problems between 1987 and 1991 and, when the theatre reopened, collapsing seats were a regular hazard for patrons. The refurbished theatre, complete with a remodelled auditorium and 616 new seats, opened in October 1996.

1997 Oxford Castle reverts to Oxfordshire County Council; John Cann, Governor of Bullingdon Prison, hands the keys over to David Buckle, Chair of Oxfordshire County Council (centre) and Chief Executive, John Harwood (left). Oxford Prison finally closed in 1996 and the County Council was able to buy back the historic site at the Victorian selling price, £9,009.

1997 The Candyskins play for customers at the HMV store in Cornmarket Street. The Oxford music scene has become very lively in recent years and Radiohead, Supergrass and Ride are among the other local bands that have achieved major international success.

1998   Russell Acott's music shop in High Street, one of Oxford's apparently permanent institutions. James Russell's music business dated back to 1811 and Sydney Acott's to 1893; the two firms merged in the 1950s. The business moved to new premises in Botley in 1999 and the old shop, like many other city centre properties, was converted into a bar.

1998   The perfume counter at Debenham's store in Magdalen Street. Debenham's took over Elliston & Cavell Ltd, the old-established department store, in 1953 but retained the old trading name until 1973. The Victorian and Edwardian buildings were ill-adapted to modern retailing and, following the closure of the store in 1999, the huge site was redeveloped behind retained façades.

1998 Protesters cling to the remains of a tree and sit tight on a chimney stack as police and bailiffs bring the occupation of the former London, Midland & Scottish Railway station to an end. Plans to widen Park End Street as part of the Oxford Transport Strategy caused enormous controversy and the old station, a Grade II* listed building, was eventually relocated to Quainton Railway Centre in Buckinghamshire.

1999 Pedestrians jostle with buses in Cornmarket in May, a few days before the launch of the Oxford Transport Strategy cleared buses from the street. Most vehicles were excluded from Cornmarket Street as long ago as 1969 but shoppers still had to contend with buses, vehicles emerging from side streets and occasional cars driven by bemused visitors.

1999 Comparative peace returns to The High as workmen complete roadworks outside University College. A police constable stands ready to reinforce the message of the U-turn sign which applies during the day to all traffic except buses, taxis and bikes. High Street has probably not been so quiet since the days of wartime petrol rationing.

Acknowledgements and Picture Credits

Most of the pictures in this book, particularly those illustrating Oxford in the first half of the century, are from the Oxfordshire History Centre, Oxfordshire County Council, and I am most grateful to my former colleague, Nuala la Vertue, for her help in tracing some of the more elusive images. Many of the images held by the Oxfordshire History Centre are now available online at http://www.pictureoxon.com. For further information about the Oxfordshire History Centre's images and other collections, please visit the Centre at St Luke's Church, Temple Road, Cowley, Oxford, OX4 2HT, telephone 01865 398200 or email oxhist@oxfordshire.gov.uk.

The Library of Newsquest Oxfordshire Ltd includes many thousands of fascinating photographs of local people, places and topics taken by photographers of the *Oxford Mail* and the *Oxford Times*, especially since the 1950s. I am indebted to Margaret Orme, Associate Editor at Newsquest, and to the Picture Editor, Keith Price, for access to the library and for permission to use copyright images whether retained by Newsquest or deposited with Oxfordshire County Council. Angela Langridge, the Librarian at Newsquest, was most helpful in facilitating my visits and in finding photographs to illustrate particular themes.

I am also grateful to Gillian Bardsley, Archivist at the British Motor Industry Heritage Trust, to Ian Carter from the Photographic Archive at the Imperial War Museum and to Jeremy Daniel of Jeremy's Oxford Stamp Centre for permission to reproduce their photographs.

British Motor Industry Heritage Trust: 23 bottom, 42 top, 51 top, 60 top

Jeremy Daniel: 37 top

Imperial War Museum: 72 top

Newsquest Oxfordshire Ltd: half title page, 2, title page, 53 bottom, 62–3, 70 top, 79 middle, 81–3, 86–7, 88 bottom, 89–90, 91 bottom, 92, 93 top, 94–5, 96 top, middle, 97 top, bottom, 100, 101 middle, bottom, 103 top, 104–6, 108, 109 top, 110, 112–14, 115 top, 116–17, back endpaper

Oxfordshire History Centre, Oxfordshire County Council: front endpaper, 6, 16–22, 23 top, 24–36, 37 bottom, 38–41, 42 bottom, 43–50, 51 middle, bottom, 52, 53 top, 54–9, 61, 64–9, 70 bottom, 71, 72 bottom, 73–8, 79 top, bottom, 80, 84–5, 88 top, 91 top, 93 bottom, 96 bottom, 97 middle, 98–9, 101 top, 102, 103 bottom, 107, 109 bottom, 111, 115 bottom, 118–20